Trees of Brundall and Braydeston:

and the stories surrounding them

Text by John Fleetwood
Photographs by Michael Foster

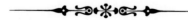

Published by Brundall Local History Group
in 2012

This book is sponsored by Brundall Homehardware
to whom we extend our grateful thanks.

Cover: 'The Roman Dock' at Brundall Gardens
Photo: Gerry Hawkins

Prepared for publication by Wendy Ward for BLHG

www.brundallarchive.co.uk

ISBN 978-0-9570689-1-9

Printed by INTERPRINT
280 Fifers Lane, Norwich, Norfolk, NR6 6EQ.

CONTENTS

Page i   Contents

Page ii   Acknowledgements

Page iii   Profile of John Fleetwood

Page viii   Frontispiece: Map showing the position of the trees

Page   3   1. The Margery Palmer Oak

Page 13   2. The Braydeston Hills Oak

Page 19   3. The Rectory Oak

Page 27   4. The Parish Boundary Oaks

Page 35   5. The Lavender House Robinia

Page 41   6. The Brundall House Trees

Page 51   7. The William Coleman Limes

Page 57   8. The Princess Diana Tree

Page 67   9. Brundall Gardens

Page 75   10. Brundall's Oak

Page 83   11. Brundall Church Fen Local Nature Reserve

Page 91   12. From our Archives

ACKNOWLEDGEMENTS

- Brundall Local History Group is very grateful to John Fleetwood for allowing us to use his eleven leaflets entitled 'The notable trees of Brundall' which he produced some time ago while he was Parish Tree Warden. His knowledge of trees in Brundall is second to none.

- We are also indebted to Michael Foster for his expertise in photographing the trees in the summer and winter. Some of them were difficult to get close to and look very dissimilar in the different seasons of the year.

- The cover photograph and most of those in the final part 'From our Archives' are by Gerry Hawkins. We thank him for his permission to use them.

- As usual, Barbara Ayers has been a tower of strength and was very supportive in getting the book ready for publication.

Wendy Ward

October 2012

PROFILE OF JOHN FLEETWOOD

In May 1985 John Fleetwood moved to Brundall from Milton Keynes with his young family to take up a new job with a Norwich engineering company. It was very soon after that he began his now infamous association with Brundall's trees!

Soon after moving into his new house on the Dales estate he learned of plans to build two houses on land at the rear of his property, land that he understood was to be preserved as woodland. He embarked on his first 'save the trees' mission. He had always loved trees and woodlands and he was to learn very quickly that his love was really a deeply held passion. He set-up the Oakhill Trust with his neighbours and successfully fought the planning application. That, in turn, led to them purchasing the site and, in so doing, securing the future of a very important small copse containing several fine mature trees. John then set about acquiring the knowledge necessary to manage such a site, although he had already learned something very valuable. A Tree Preservation Order does not prevent a tree being cut down. It may give the tree the status as being worthy of preservation but it does not give it immunity to the chainsaw!

With the help of Broadland District Council's Arboricultural Officer at that time, Margaret MacQueen, and local tree surgeons, particularly Nick Coleman and Colin McDonald of Tree Care, plus some locally held courses, John soon found that he had become quite knowledgeable about trees and arboriculture. Indeed, in 1996, when Brundall Parish Council advertised the position of Parish Tree Warden, he felt equipped to carry out the duties. He applied and was duly appointed.

Becoming a Parish Tree Warden meant that John could take more courses and meet more people from whom he could learn and he was soon regarded as being 'very knowledgeable' about the subject. The first 'event' he organised was the planting of a cherry tree in the shopper's car park on The Street to celebrate the life of Diana Princess of Wales. The planting, in March 1998, was very well attended by both parishioners and local dignitaries. The Reverend Richard Espin-Bradley of St Laurence Church dedicated

John Fleetwood leading a walk by Brundall Local History Group 21st June 2011
speaking about the Robinia tree outside The Lavender House

the tree during a short service.

Having always had an interest in writing and having the computer skills necessary to produce leaflets, etc, John started to produce a series of leaflets about the Notable Trees of Brundall (on which this book is based) and that led directly to Broadland District Council's Arboricultural Officer asking him to produce a monthly newsletter for the Broadland Parish Tree Wardens.

Those of you who know him will not be surprised to learn that he wasn't satisfied with a simple newsletter but he now produces a monthly twenty page colour magazine for Tree Wardens not only in Broadland but also across the country, plus overseas. He recently produced the one hundredth issue and Broadland District Council marked the milestone with the presentation of a book voucher with which he purchased a couple of text books on … trees!!

In 1999, he embarked on the creation of our much loved and much acclaimed Brundall Church Fen Local Nature Reserve. Initially, he worked very closely with Eilish Rothney of the Broads Authority, someone who he credits with having taught him a great deal. She encouraged him to broaden his learning base and obtain more skills, which he did. Most important though, Eilish gave him the self-confidence necessary to undertake major projects and voice his opinions on conservation matters.

It was Eilish who encouraged John to start a series of walks through the village for parishioners, telling them about our trees, their history and how studying them can reveal more details of the history of Brundall. She also encouraged him to begin the annual Church Fen Local Nature Reserve Open Days which attracted around 100 visitors each year and were most enjoyable. The free boats trips across to Surlingham were always fully booked!!

After some time Eilish moved to pastures new and was replaced by Lee Harris who continued to give the help and advice that Eilish had provided in the past. Indeed, it was Lee who eventually approached Norfolk County Council about the chances of achieving Local Nature Reserve status.

Heidi Mahon from Norfolk County Council handled the application process with English Nature (now Natural England) and after some time the site was given Local Nature Reserve status. It was a great achievement for Brundall Parish Council and the grand opening was a great day for John. He invited Lee and Heidi to officially open the new Local Nature Reserve and, in his speech, he thanked them and Eilish Rothney for all the help they had given him.

Perhaps the highlight of the 15 years he served as Brundall's Parish Tree Warden was the surprise award he received on behalf of Brundall Parish

Council from the Campaign for the Protection of Rural England Conservation Award for the creation and management of the Local Nature Reserve that meant so much to him.

A common question he has answered is "which is your favourite tree species?" Without hesitation he answers the English oak because he regards it as an icon of England and it displays power, majesty and beauty.

Another question he is often asked is "which is your favourite tree in Brundall?"

"That is not quite so straightforward as each can make its own claim" he answers. "The Lavender House Robinia is so old for the species and it is amazing it found its way here and the Princess Diana tree has great meaning. However, I guess my favourite is the Margery Palmer Oak. It is an English oak and is named after such a wonderful lady who gave so much of herself to help others. Then, in that terrible lightning strike, the tree was so badly damaged and scarred but the view that she enjoyed so much from her window was unscathed. Amazing."

John is always eager to explain that without the national Tree Warden Scheme, organised by the Tree Council and administered locally by Broadland District Council, none of what he has done would have been possible. It is a purely voluntary role but full training is given on a range of topics from the administration of Tree Preservation Orders to hedge laying and from tree identification to the provision of wetland habitats. He is a fervent supporter of the scheme and, as you can imagine, is one of the most 'involved' of Broadland's Wardens, not least of all because he produces their magazine.

He is keen to point out that local authorities have a most difficult role to play in dealing with trees. He says that conversations with the public always start with "I love trees, but that one at the bottom of my garden...". On the other hand, the public have no idea what it costs to create a Tree Preservation Order and are critical if the local authority doesn't throw them around like confetti.

He cannot give enough praise and sincere thanks to Broadland District Council's Conservation Officer, Barbara Hornbrook, and their Arboricultural Officer, Steve Chesney-Beales, plus everyone in the Conservation team. They give so much help and advice and are always there to support Tree Wardens whenever needed. They have built a first-class Tree Warden Scheme, one of the best in the country, and John says that the public have no idea of what a debt they owe those officers of the Council.

He also carries out voluntary work for the Woodland Trust, our leading conservation charity, and is a Voluntary Speaker, travelling far and wide (from Manchester to south London) giving talks to organisations from the local WI to major conservation charities etc. In addition, he gives talks to schools at any opportunity offered to him because he believes that it is only by educating children and showing them nature at first hand that we can have any hope of preserving it.

Over the years he served as Brundall Parish Tree Warden, John gave help and advice to all who asked for it … and it was free of charge! Of course, not everyone agreed with his opinion when he told them that he could not justify the felling of a particular tree. However, as much as they may have disagreed with his opinion, they couldn't question his passion for the protection of our trees.

John has now moved on to pastures new and has become Parish Tree Warden for Freethorpe and Wickhampton Parish Council. We understand he is even creating a new Local Nature Reserve there.

*

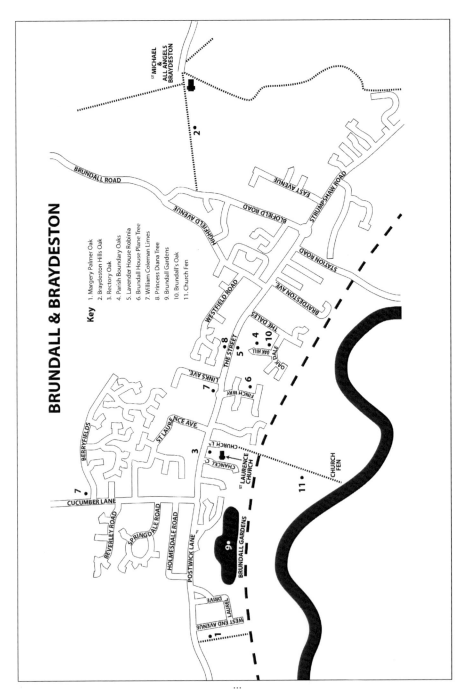

BRUNDALL & BRAYDESTON

Key
1. Margery Palmer Oak
2. Braydeston Hills Oak
3. Rectory Oak
4. Parish Boundary Oaks
5. Lavender House Robinia
6. Brundall House Plane Tree
7. William Coleman Limes
8. Princess Diana Tree
9. Brundall Gardens
10. Brundall's Oak
11. Church Fen

1

'The Margery Palmer Oak'

1

The Margery Palmer Oak

TOWARDS the western extremity of Brundall, just a couple of hundred metres inside the parish boundary, there is a most notable tree. It sits on the rear boundary of Wilby Cottage, 12 West End Avenue, alongside a lane leading to an Anglian Water Authority station and is known locally as The Margery Palmer Oak. It is a truly magnificent *pedunculate* oak *Quercus robur*, standing a full 24m in height with a girth at breast height of 4.63m. There is little doubt that it started life as a hedgerow tree, but today one can easily live in the village without being aware of its existence.

Was the tree planted or was it self-set? We can only speculate I'm afraid. As it was a constituent of a hedgerow, it is quite likely that it was planted. However, as I said, that is just speculation. Regretfully, we shall never know how it came to be there. It is between 190 and 210 years of age, by no means old by oak standards but still to be respected. It is one of the oldest oaks in Brundall today and began its life at some time between 1788 and 1808, around the time of the French Revolution. George Washington had just become the first President of the USA. The population of Brundall was just 39 with 108 in Braydeston, which at that time was a separate parish. There was no railway in the village then, the first train not passing through until 1844. In fact, at this time, Brundall was very small. The most westerly house was the cottage on the corner of Cucumber Lane; the chief concern of the villagers was agriculture and only four people (three in Brundall and one in Braydeston) were eligible to vote! It comprised just a few houses along roads which were in a deplorable condition. They were little more than muddy tracks and in winter they were often impassable. Number 12 West End Avenue, later to become Wilby Cottage, was built in 1925; some 130 years or so after that little oak seedling produced its first leaf. It was part of the original development of West End Avenue and the oak and hedgerow were included in the property as its western boundary. Needless to say, the oak was already a substantial tree when the cottage was built, so there must have been a conscious decision to retain it and incorporate it into the garden.

By that time, Brundall and Braydeston had been amalgamated as a

The Margery Palmer Oak, winter 2011-2

The Margery Palmer Oak summer 2012

This picture shows the damage done to the trunk of the oak
by the lightning strike in summer 1970

A painting of the Margery Palmer Oak by
Peter Jamieson, reproduced here by kind
permission of the artist

single parish, although the ecclesiastical parishes remained separate, and the population was around 900. It was still a small village, although its growth had begun and continued steadily from then on. The property was purchased from new by Miss Ethel and Miss Helen Colman of Carrow Abbey, members of the Norwich Colman family famed for its mustard. In 1923-24, the Misses Colman were respectively Lord Mayor and Lady Mayoress of Norwich. Miss Ethel died in 1948 at the age of 85 and Miss Helen in 1947 aged 82. However, the Colman sisters only ever actually lived in the property during World War II when they evacuated themselves to the cottage from Norwich, catching the early train into the city every day and returning by teatime.

They actually purchased the cottage for their cousin, Miss Margery Palmer, who had been their personal secretary for many years. One of Miss Palmer's constant interests was the well being of Carrow Works' pensioners, whom she regularly visited. Miss Palmer named the property Wilby Cottage, taking the name from Wilby Hall where she was born in 1889. It was conveyed to her on 28 March 1925 and she continued to live there until her death in 1970 at the age of 81. For many years she was, among many other activities and interests, Churchwarden of the Church of St Laurence in Brundall, where she is buried.

Following Miss Margery Palmer's death, the cottage was bequeathed to Mr J L and Mrs A M Fielding who formed part of the Colman family, there having been three Fielding/Colman marriages during the nineteenth and twentieth centuries. They never actually lived in the cottage, but instead let it to eight different consecutive tenants between 1971 and August 1985, when they sold it and finally ended the Colman/Fielding links with the property.

Mr and Mrs T R Barker became the new owners of Wilby Cottage on 13 August 1985. They carried out extensive renovation works, the property having been somewhat neglected. The Barkers lived there until 1994 when it was purchased by the current owners, Tony and Liz Newsam who I must thank for their help with the history of the property.

Margery Palmer was very fond of her oak, enjoying it through the seasons for many years from her lovely cottage. It was the subject of a pen and ink drawing by Peter Jamieson, son of her neighbours Mr and Mrs W J Jamieson, who have also been the source of much information in the preparation of this leaflet. At that time, Peter was studying at the Royal Academy of Art in London and he drew the cottage and garden viewed from under the tree. Following her death, friends of Miss Margery Palmer set up a Memorial Fund and decided to erect a plaque on the tree. The bronze plaque in an oak frame carries the inscription "Margery Palmer's Oak. 'By works was faith made perfect.' 1889-1970. A tribute from family and friends." The quotation, taken from the General Epistle of James 2, verse 22, was selected by the Reverend Geoffrey Church, a former Rector of the Church of St Laurence.

Unfortunately, during the summer of 1970, before the plaque was erected, the tree was dramatically struck by lightning and suffered severe damage. At first, it appeared that it would die and would have to be felled. However, Arthur Harper of Economic Forestry Ltd. was engaged to advise on what could be done and, although he could give no guarantees on the eventual outcome, he recommended extensive tree surgery and commented that it was "one of the nicest hedgerow specimens in Norfolk". This presented a problem for those that had collected donations for the plaque as they were suddenly faced with the task of funding the tree surgery. That was when Peter Jamieson decided to make a wood-cut from his drawing of the cottage, enabling a limited number of prints to be sold in aid of the fund. That enabled the work to proceed as planned.

Mr Harper's recommendations were followed in detail and everyone was delighted when the tree burst into leaf in the following spring. There can be little doubt that Mr Harper deserves great praise for a job very well done. Today, the tree is full of vigour, although it bears the terrible scars of that lightning strike. One side has been taken away and the trunk is beginning to go hollow. Hollow oak trunks are not a weakness though. The tree does not need heartwood, that being of use to cabinet-makers and boat-builders. It lives off the sapwood only and that appears to be thriving following a successful healing process.

One final, fascinating point. If you look at the tree today from the cottage, the view that Miss Margery Palmer loved so much, you can see no sign of that lightning strike damage. Perhaps there is something in that. In an act of untold power, God preserved that treasured view. As it says on the memorial plaque, "By works was faith made perfect".

*

9

2

'The Braydeston Hills Oak'

2

The Braydeston Hills Oak

IN THE middle of Braydeston Hills, sitting in a slight hollow, is a solitary oak. It is as solitary as St Michael's Church at the top of the hill. It is a *pedunculate* oak *Quercus robur* and has a gnarled and somewhat sorry looking appearance. You often see youngsters sitting under it and dogs are always to be seen sniffing around it as this is one of the most popular dog exercise areas in the village. If you walk there during the week you may see the traditional sight of cattle seeking shade beneath it.

We all pass it quite regularly and, quite frankly, we just take it for granted. No, it doesn't look a particularly attractive tree, I suppose, but old oaks don't look particularly pretty in that sense. How old do you think it is? Have you ever considered how old it is? Does it really matter? Yes, I think it does. It is part of our heritage and has seen so much. Besides, I am sure that we would miss it very much if it were to suddenly disappear. It has become one of the landmarks of Brundall.

The Braydeston Hills Oak is only 12m (40 feet) tall but the trunk has a girth at breast height of some 4.24m (13feet 11inches). If you take time to have a closer look at it, you will see that it is almost completely hollow. Never mind that though, because a living tree does not need its heartwood as that is dead. It is the sapwood that is the living part and in the case of the Braydeston Hills Oak that is very much alive. The tree shows evidence of having been pollarded at one time. Pollarding was carried out at regular intervals in order to provide fuel wood. Taking its girth and allowing for the fact that it is a pollard, I should estimate that this tree is between 160 and 190 years of age. By oak standards, this is not an old tree. Oaks can live for 900 years. However, it is not only age which makes a tree important. This is one of Brundall's landmarks and compared with other trees in the village it is old. So, the Braydeston Hills Oak began life between 1808 and 1838. It was around the time of the Retreat from Moscow and the destruction of Napoleon's Grand Army. It could have been the same year as the death of Napoleon or the death of King George III. At that time, Braydeston was still a

The Braydeston Hills Oak March 2012

totally separate parish from Brundall and had a population between 108 and 142, Brundall having just 55 residents. Was the tree planted or was it self-set? This is always a difficult question. Why would someone plant a single oak in the middle of a field? How would a single oak seedling survive in the middle of a field? Who knows? I guess we could speculate, but I see no real value in that. Let's just be thankful that it is there and enjoy it while we can.

As I said earlier, the Braydeston Hills Oak and St Michael's Church occupy a lonely setting on Braydeston Hills. However, it wasn't always like that. There was a church there in Saxon times and there are traces of Saxon work in the south wall. Nevertheless, most of the present building dates from around 1450. The remote setting is probably due to the fact that the village, which one would expect to see surrounding its church, moved away after the Black Death of 1349.

Looking at the ground surrounding the tree, it has always been well used. Whether it be young boys, young girls, courting couples, senior citizens taking a breather or meeting for a chat, inquisitive canine visitors from terriers to great danes, or just the cattle during the week. It is the cattle that have helped to provide us with the ready-made seat at the base of the tree. For years they have scraped their feet on the base as they have tried to browse on the lower foliage and the tree has repaired that damage by callusing over the wounds. Over the years the calluses have become very large and today provide a seat around the base of the tree.

Inside too, the tree has been very well used. An oak can support some 423 different species of insect and mite. They have all used it, some spending their whole lives on or in the tree. In turn, of course, birds visit the tree to feed on the insects and mites and so the system goes on. Even the rotting inside of the tree has supported wood boring beetles, wood-rotting fungi, etc.. During its lifetime, the Braydeston Hills oak has supported literally millions of other forms of life.

So, how much longer will it serve as such a landmark to us? Who can tell? A lightning strike could mark its end tomorrow. Life is that tenuous. 160 years of history can easily be ended in twenty minutes with a chain saw. That is why I find our old trees so wonderful. OK, this is not an ancient oak as you would see at the Felbrigg and Blickling estates. Some of those are more than three times the age of our Braydeston Hills Oak. Nevertheless, if this was a person who had lived for the best part of two centuries we would think it a wonderful achievement. So let's not take these old trees for granted. I have a photograph of the Braydeston Hills Oak, taken on a bright, sunny day with cattle beneath its canopy. It is in my file as a permanent record of this lovely old village landmark. In my memory though, I will always retain the sight of a retired gentleman sitting on one of the lower outgrowths of the tree, resting with his hands on his knees as his equally senior German shepherd dog sniffed around inquisitively. After some time the gentleman got up, called his faithful friend and started his return walk home. He would repeat the process tomorrow, just as he did yesterday and the day before that. The tree had great meaning to them both.

So the next time you walk across Braydeston Hills, just take the time to look at the tree and think a little of what it has seen. Enjoy the Braydeston Hills Oak.

*

Here is the Braydeston Hills Oak in a winter scene
showing its relationship to Braydeston Church
(photo: Gerry Hawkins)

3

'The Rectory Oak'

3

The Rectory Oak

ONE of the delights of our village is the wonderful tree canopy to be enjoyed as you pass along The Street. As I drive home from the office each evening and turn that sharp left hand corner from Cucumber Lane into The Street, I find that view along past the church quite wonderful. Each season brings its own breathtaking qualities. It always displays something different, but always remains a lovely scene, somehow taking the stress of the day away.

One of the major constituents of that canopy is The Rectory Oak. Sited on the front boundary of The Rectory, this *pedunculate* oak *Quercus robur*, dominates the sky line, its boughs reaching across to the opposite side of the road and its foliage giving that unique lighting effect that only an English oak can. It gives The Street a green roof. What a combination the oak is. The power and dominance of its overall form. The immense strength revealed by that trunk and the larger of the limbs. Those shapes which gave the Armada its fighting ships. All that power and yet the foliage is somehow delicate. It gives rise to those wonderful dappled lighting effects. That evening sunlight flickering through those famously shaped leaves. It's so..............so..............so England!

The Rectory Oak stands 15 m (50 feet) tall and the trunk has a girth of 4.11 m (13 feet 6inches). It is a fine, stately tree between 167 and 187 years old and totally dominates that section of the village. Now, they say that an oak spends 300 years growing old, rests for 300 years and then spends 300 years gracefully retiring. If that is the case, then The Rectory Oak is just a youngster. Nevertheless, this tree has seen quite a few changes during its lifetime. Let us just consider a few of them. It was planted around 1811, during the reign of King George III and the year of the Luddite riots. It was just a couple of inches tall at the time of the Battle of Waterloo and the assassination of Prime Minister Spencer Percival. The population of Brundall was a mere 55, although we should add the 108 in Braydeston as that was classed as a separate parish in those days. A total population of just 163! It

The Rectory Oak March 2012

must have been a lonely old existence being a young tree at that time. Of course, the immediate vicinity of the tree was totally different then. The Rectory had not been built, the Old Rectory being on the opposite side of the road where it survives today. Opposite the church, in front of the row of cottages, was a village green and pond. That was the heart of the village at that time. In addition, the edge of the road on the opposite side to the church was positioned about where the centre of the road is today. All the subsequent road widening over the years has been done on the northern side, which is why there are no old trees bounding that side of The Street. The lovely churchyard of St Laurence Church would have been more visible than it is today and, of course, you would have probably been able to see the church itself from The Street.

As The Rectory Oak is part of the church, perhaps we should look at some of the history of that fine building. The earliest part dates from about 1250 AD. There is no tower, but a small double bell turret containing a single bell dated 1778. A north aisle was added in 1900 and a year later a porch. The 13th century lead cased font is the only one in the country. The Old Rectory, on the opposite side of The Street, was built by the Reverend John Russell in about 1705, but has not been a rectory since 1799.

Not only has The Rectory Oak seen many changes in the establishment of Brundall, but its immediate environment has changed dramatically. Some of those changes must have seriously threatened the tree's survival from time to time. When it began life, The Street was nothing more than a muddy track, probably impassable in bad weather. The population of 163 moved about basically on foot. Yes, people thought nothing of walking three or four miles in those days, whereas today we get in our cars to travel from Cucumber Lane or Blofield Road to the shops in the centre of the village. There was no long line of cars parked outside the church on a Sunday morning in those days! Maybe one or two travelled by horse drawn carriage and some on horse back, but there were definitely no cars.

Over the years, The Rectory Oak has had to learn to live with the pollution of the internal combustion engine replacing the fresher, cleaner air of the last century. With that, of course, go the regular doses of road salt we give it during the winter. Oh yes, it's so easy to overlook that isn't it? That road salt that the County Council kindly puts on our roads during winter gets splashed against The Rectory Oak and it has had to learn to survive that. When you consider what that salt does to the surface of the road, not to mention your car bodywork, it is a miracle that the tree has survived at all.

Nevertheless, despite all that modern man has thrown at it, The Rec-

The Rectory Oak August 2012

tory Oak still holds pride of place along The Street. It stands there night and day, summer and winter, through drought, flood and gales. It survives the polluted air and the road salt and remains majestic, dominating the area and providing that wonderful canopy that only an oak can. The base displays lichens which use the tree as a host. Just look at the subtle changes in their colour as you travel from the base, up the trunk. Meanwhile modern Brundall man uses that trunk as a notice board. Where would the playgroup be without the free advertising afforded by The Rectory Oak? Where would all the other organisations be if they could not use this 187 year old free notice board? Just how many drawing pins are there inside that tree today? Now there's an idea for a competition. How many drawing pins are there on The Rectory Oak? I think that this is a wonderful tree and so very interesting and I trust that the Parish Tree Warden in another 187 years will still be enjoying The Rectory Oak.

*

4

'The Parish Boundary
Oaks'

4

The Parish Boundary Oaks

NOTABLE trees do not have to be single trees or very old trees, very tall trees or very broad trees, unusual trees or outstanding trees. There are many things which can make a tree interesting. The Parish Boundary Oaks are interesting because they are the remnants of a locally important line of oaks, marking the old parish boundary between Brundall and Braydeston.

Brundall and Braydeston were separate parishes until their amalgamation in 1883. Their original common boundary was marked by a line of *pedunculate Quercus robur*, stretching from the railway, north through what is today The Dales estate and up to the rear of the properties on the southern side of The Street. There were originally around 27 of them, but sadly only 7 survive today and 3 of those are displaying bracket fungi which herald the demise of a tree. The trees vary somewhat in size, but we have to assume that were all planted at the same time. Try as I may, I cannot find any record of when exactly they were planted, so I have had to calculate their age from their girth and the growth conditions. From that, I believe that we are safe to assume that the boundary was planted up in around 1828, making the trees around 172 years old.

So, what changes have these trees experienced during their lifetime? The time of planting coincides with the deaths of Beethoven and Chaka, the great Zulu warrior. It was the year before the Metropolitan Police Force was established and a couple of years before the death of King George IV. Brundall had a population of 63 and about a dozen houses. Braydeston had 145 residents in 28 houses. So, we have a total population of 208 inhabiting some 40 houses. A little different from today! Of course, the boundary was planted up some 16 years before the first train passed through Brundall and it could have been that the trees extended down to the river. However, I think that would have been highly unlikely due to the marshy nature of the ground. Maybe there were one or two more trees in the line, but no more than that. Moreover, one would expect to see survivors south of the railway rather than the north because all the development of the village has been to the north. Today, three of the survivors are in local authority ownership, two are in private gardens and the other two are on undeveloped private land. Thankfully, all are protected by Tree Preservation Orders. As I said earlier, three of the surviving trees are displaying bracket fungi. In recent years, Broadland District Council has carried out a major crown reduction on each of them and, although it cannot save them, it should delay the inevitable day when the chainsaw ends their lives.

During the last decade, two others have fallen to the chainsaw. One due to fungal disease and another due to becoming unsafe following a lightning strike. In each case, a replacement was planted nearby, but it will be another eighty years or so before they begin to impose themselves on the landscape. Only then will they be able to assume a proper place among their peers.

The seven surviving Parish Boundary Oaks range from 12 to 15m (40 to 50 feet) in height and are between 2.87 and 4.06m (9 feet 5 inches -13 feet 4 inches) in girth. They vary from a majestic, domineering tree on the front garden of number 9 Oakhill, to a fairly sorry looking specimen on the land awaiting development adjacent to the railway. They include a tree on the amenity land in Oakhill which has a hollow trunk and it is quite interesting to take a look inside a see just how a tree works.

There is ample evidence of Neolithic or New Stone Age occupation of part of Brundall and tools
dating from around 3500 BC have been found. The earliest remains recorded in Braydeston were a number of Romano-British cremation urns, found in about 1820 on the corner of Station Road and Station New Road. A Saxon site was unearthed at "Watermeadows" in Station New Road in 1932. The Domesday Book of 1086 almost always provides the first description of any parish. The entries for Brundall and Braydeston read as follows:-

Brundale

On the expulsion of Godwin, a freeman, who had a carucate of land under the protection of Guert, the Conqueror, on his accession to the Crown, gave it to Ralph de Guaeder, Earl of Norfolk who was deprived as a rebel and at the Survey, Gilbert Captain of the cross-bowmen held it with two carucates of land when there were five borders with a carucate in demesne and the men always ploughed their land with two oxen, pannage for five swine and 25 acres of meadow, 12½ freemen possessed 90 acres of land with a carucate and a half valued formerly at 25/- now 49/-. It was one luca long and one and a half broad and paid 7/- geld. Gilbert was also Lord of

Tunstall in Walsham Hundred. Note: The half freeman would also hold land in another manor, probably Braydeston where there was also a half freeman.

Braydeston

Land of the Bishop of Thetford belonging to his fee in "Blafelda" Hundred. In "Bregestuna" a freeman, Edric, Captain of King Edward's ship, one carucate of land. Always four villeins and one bordar, and two servi. And three acres of meadows. Always one plough in the demesne; and half a plough of the tenants. Pannage for two hogs and always one carthorse and six head of cattle and sixty sheep. Now sixteen hogs and sixteen goats. A church of ten acres and worth 10d. To this belongs ten freemen and a half, his predecessor had only the protection of eighty acres of land. Three acres of meadow. Always two ploughs. And in the same 'B'lingham' four acres and a half of land belonging to Brerestuna. Then worth 10/- and afterwards the same, now (the survey) 30/- and after King William came to England this Edric was banished into Dacia and Almar usurped the land. William de Noer now holds it.

The churches of the two parishes, the Church of St Lawrence in Brundall and Braydeston St Michael are described in the leaflets covering the Rectory Oak and the Braydeston Hills Oak respectively. For 800 years, from the Domesday Book in 1086 to the amalgamation of the two parishes in 1883, the population of Brundall varied between 39 and 104. It is strange to note that there was more than double the number of people in the parish at the time of Domesday than in 1801 and almost double the number than in 1841. It is also surprising to find that the population had almost recovered by 1381, only 32 years after the Black Death which was reputed to have almost halved the population in this part of the country.

Of course, for many years these trees looked across at Brundall House and its surrounding land. For so many years the most important house in Brundall, it is sad that it has now passed into history. There are a few remnants of its former glory. The small copse at the rear of the properties in Oakhill was planted as part of the grounds of the house and I am pleased to say that it is now preserved. There is also the area of trees at the bottom of the Finch Way development, adjacent to the railway, which is also preserved but is suffering from damage.

A third remnant of Brundall House is the avenue of limes at the top of Berryfields. That is the subject of number 6 in this series of leaflets. In 1948, the Church Commissioners proposed that the ecclesiastical parish of Braydeston, which had previously been merged with that of Strumpshaw, should be joined to the parishes of Brundall and Witton. It was also proposed that Braydeston Church should become a chapel of ease. Needless to say, that proposal was strongly rejected by the Braydeston parishioners. The only appeal against the findings of the Commissioners is to the Judicial Committee of the Privy Council. Therefore, a fund was set up to finance what would be an expensive procedure. £266 was soon raised and the services of Mr Quintin Hogg as counsel were secured.

The hearing took place on 16 and 17 May 1950 at 11 Downing Street and in their judgment, delivered on 10 July 1950, the Court ordered that the amalgamation of the three parishes should stand, but that Braydeston should remain a distinct parish with its church fully operational. Mr Quintin Hogg waived nearly all of his fee. It is possible that The Parish Boundary Oaks were originally constituents of a hedgerow, but I can find no evidence to support that. In any case, that is long gone now.

Although some of these trees are dying, several have been felled and there is very little of the original boundary surviving, the trees are, in their final years, providing the next generation of Brundall oaks. In a wonderful project, funded by Broadland District Council and given the full support of Brundall Parish Council, children from Brundall County Primary School collected acorns from these trees and are now raising seedlings to be planted out in the Millennium. Those same children will plant the trees out around the village and the trees will carry plates specifying the names of those who raised and planted them. The children will then be encouraged to care for the saplings, keeping them free from weeds and ensuring that they will grow into trees worthy of their parents. This project, named The Brundall Millennium Tree Planting Project, has gained widespread acclaim, but would not have been possible without the full co-operation of David Capp, the Headmaster at that time. During the next year, these seedlings will be complemented by some raised by the Cubs and Scouts. The youth of the village will be raising the trees for their generation and the next from those of our generation and the past. The Parish Boundary Oaks will live on through their off-spring and will continue to give pleasure to the people of Brundall for many years to come.

Finally, The Parish Boundary Oaks have given rise to two most suitable road names. In these days when road names seem to have little local significance, but instead reflect the political bias of the government of the day, be it national or local, it is refreshing that Oakhill and Oakdale Road are so named. Maybe you failed to realise that The Parish Boundary Oaks gave rise to these names. The trees will live on in the names of these roads, assuming of course that the man made environment can last as long as the natural one!

On a personal note, I have the privilege of being able to look out of my study window upon these majestic trees. As I am writing this, I turn my head to the right and see two of the best of the survivors. What better place for a Parish Tree Warden to live? Oakhill with The Parish Boundary Oaks.

*

5

'The Lavender House
Robinia'

5

The Lavender House Robinia

THE Lavender House Restaurant, formerly the Old Beams Restaurant, has become a landmark in Brundall. How lucky we are to have such a high quality establishment in the village. The warm welcome from the proprietors, the culinary genius producing such wonderful food, the first class service and the unique atmosphere where everyone is made to feel so welcome, makes it a very special venue.

The building dates from the seventeenth century and has retained its thatched roof and old world character. It was, as far back as the early seventeen hundreds, Braydeston "White Horse", the village pub. In May 1741 a camping match was advertised in a Norwich newspaper to take place there. In 1880, the licence was transferred to the present White Horse public house at the eastern end of the Street. Sadly, that closed its doors for the last time during 2000.

Although we pass it nearly every day, many of us fail to notice the oldest tree in the village sitting on the right hand side of the building. It may look like a withered thing, not that big and therefore probably not that old, but just how wrong can you be? The tree, a *Robinia, Robinia pseudoacacia* (also known as false acacia or locust tree), is reported to be 250 years old. Now it is extremely difficult to age these trees They are a bit like yew in that respect, often being considerably older than they appear. It is beyond my knowledge to disagree with that estimate of the tree's age (made by a botanist from Kew Gardens) and I have to accept the figure I have been given. I have discussed the matter with several eminent "tree people", who assure me that such an age is more than possible.

So, this tree was planted around 1750, during the reign of George II. Henry Pelham was Prime Minister and it was a few years after the Jacobites were destroyed by Cumberland at Culloden. The composer J S Bach died in 1750 and it was 26 years before the American Declaration of Independence. I wonder just how many of those events, which today we class as important historical dates, really made any difference to the people of Brundall at that time. How long did it take for the news to actually reach them?

The population of Brundall and Braydeston in 1750 is not known as the first census was not until 1801 when Brundall had just 39 residents. No figures are available for Braydeston until 1811 when they counted 108. That makes a total population of just 147 compared with today's figure of over 4,000. The *Robinia* is a native of the Appalachian Mountains in North America, although it has since run wild from southern Canada to California. It's Latin name means false acacia and that is often used as a common name for the tree.

British colonists at Jamestown discovered the species in 1607 and it was introduced to Britain in 1636. It enjoyed a brief period of popularity, but was then forgotten until about 1820 when William Cobbett began importing saplings from the USA, proclaiming that the timber would become more popular than oak. Although there was an immediate response and Cobbett sold over a million trees, the popularity was short-lived. The tree was first mentioned growing in Britain in a book called "Theatre of Plants" by Parkinson in 1640. The timber is particularly strong, resistant to rot and very heavy and was first imported to Britain for ship building. It is well-grained, brown and lasts longer than oak when used as a fence post. It often appears in poetry because nightingales liked to sing from *Robinia* trees and it is thought that nightingales nested in *robinias* because the thorns protected them from their enemies. Could it be that the nightingale that sang in Berkeley Square in the famous song was sitting in a *Robinia*? The flowers are a good source of food for honey bees. All parts of the tree are poisonous to humans. Splinters can cause blood poisoning. It thrives in pollution and likes a well-drained, light, sandy soil. It has no insect value but has a fair value to birds.

Returning to the time that the tree was planted, picture Brundall. Rural England. A thatched pub serving a small village along a muddy track. We can take the average household as being a mother, father and three children at that time. The children were too young to visit the pub and, of course, women didn't go there either. That leaves just 20% of the population, 29 men, who may have been customers at the Old Beams. Of those 29 men, some would never be seen in such a place, so let's say that the old Beams pub has a total of, at most, 20 customers. So, a traditional pub, log fire, tankards of the local brew and at most 20 customers, the greater majority of whom probably never travelled more than ten miles from Brundall in their whole lives.......................and someone plants this North American tree outside! Why? It is totally inexplicable. Of course, we shall never know why

The Lavender House Robinia August 2012

and perhaps that's why history is so fascinating. You can get most of the facts, but every now and again you have to use your imagination. Perhaps it was a bit like people planting *Leylandii* today.

Today, The Old Beams *Robinia* is probably Brundall's only true veteran tree and is very old for the species in Britain. As such, we must value it and pay it the respect it deserves. Perhaps we should begin to consider what it would be like to lose it. I believe that it will have a great effect on the character of the building should it disappear. Old buildings somehow need to be surrounded by old trees. When it eventually goes, will a replacement be planted? Can it be replaced? How do you suddenly replace a quarter of a century of village history? How many people have walked past it in that quarter of a century? Would it be 500,000? A million maybe? How can we possibly guess? It has lived through two World Wars, several droughts, and quite a few gales. It has endured scorching sun and spent many nights in sub-zero temperatures. It has spanned three or four generations and still goes on. It has watched this village of ours grow into what it is today. I find that simply incredible.

One of the delights in life, as far as I am concerned, is to enjoy a Sunday roast in that superb restaurant and then be able to admire, maybe even put my arms around, The Old Beams *Robinia* as I leave for home to sleep off my indulgences.

*

6

'The Brundall House Trees'

6

The Brundall House Trees

FOR many years, the most important house in the parish was Brundall House and, as such, it has left its mark on the village with several remnants still to be found. Brundall House was sited where the Finch Way estate is today and was built by Elisha de Hague in about 1815-20. Born in 1754 of a Huguenot family of grocers who settled in the parish of St Augustine Norwich, his father, also Elisha de Hague, was Town Clerk of Norwich. Elisha junior followed his father into the office of Town Clerk following Elisha senior's death in 1792 and also carried on the practice of attorney in Elm Hill. De Hague owned property in Brundall as early as 1802 for he voted as a freeholder there in the 1802 election. When Brundall Common was enclosed in 1814-16, he was the third largest claimant with seventeen going rights. In 1825 he sat for a portrait by Sir William Beechey which is now in St Andrew's Hall. A small portrait of him was painted by W Wilton and engraved by W C Edwards, but the whereabouts of that original picture is not known.

Elisha de Hague died in Brundall House on 11 November 1826 and is buried in the churchyard of St Augustine's Norwich. Following his death, the house was purchased by the Reverend Lambert Blackwell Foster who sold it in about 1848 to Henry Chamberlin, founder of the Norwich drapery firm. It is probable that Chamberlain extended the house on its western end. It is interesting to note that when the 1851 census was taken, it was found that eighteen persons had slept in Brundall House on the previous night. That will give an indication of its size. In 1864, Robert John Harvey DL purchased the property and he, in turn, sold it to Edward Trafford in 1875. Then in 1896 Brundall House was bought by William Coleman who is the subject of Chapter 7, The William Coleman Limes. As a result, I will not dwell on him now. Suffice to say, William Coleman invented Wincarnis in 1887. As well as purchasing Brundall House, he also acquired much land in Brundall. However, in 1900 he became financially involved and his trustees sold the house to Henry ffiske. Coleman's finances recovered and in 1906 he re-purchased the house from Henry ffiske at a higher price than he sold it. However, his recovery was short-lived and further financial troubles forced him to sell it again.

Between 1914 and 1918, the years of World War I, the house was used as a military hospital. It must have been a far cry from those early days. The grandeur of the de Hague era, the Chamberlins and Coleman was suddenly replaced with the brutal results of trench warfare. That appears to have marked the end of the grand days of Brundall House. In 1919 it became Miss Rivet's School and then in 1925 it again changed hands, being acquired by Herbert King Finch who owned the property until 1941 when it again came under military occupation. The end of World War II saw Mrs Wightman purchase the house and she continued in ownership until she sold it to a developer who, on 11 November 1969, sadly demolished it to make way for today's Finch Way estate, thereby ending a major chapter in the history of Brundall.

When Elisha de Hague built the house, the combined population of Brundall and Braydeston was around 170. It was just before the death of King George IV and Napoleon was keeping an engagement at Waterloo. It was some 25 years or so before the first train passed through the village. When the house was demolished, the population had risen to somewhere between 1,500 and 2,000 and, as well as defeating Napoleon, we had successfully fought two world wars in which Brundall House had played a significant role. Needless to say, the grounds of Brundall House were extensive, even without William Coleman's temporary extension. Many trees were planted within those grounds, but today just a few remain. It is most important that the survivors are preserved and afforded their full value.

The majority of those survivors are to be found in Oakhill Wood. When the Dales estate was built, Broadland District Council insisted that Wilcon Homes retain the small woodland intact as an amenity area. Since then, it has passed into the ownership of the Oakhill Trust, of which I am a Trustee, and its preservation is now guaranteed. Although access is now restricted, visitors are welcome if they contact me in advance. Many trees were preserved when Finch Way was built, but all too many have rapidly disappeared over the years and few of the specimen trees now survive. It is a perfect example of the fact that a Tree Preservation Order does not actually prevent a tree being lost.

So, what can we find of these trees? Beginning in Oakhill Wood, there are three outstanding trees. Firstly, there is a fine pedunculate oak *Quercus robur*, 15 m or so in height with a girth of 2.85 m. It is about 130 years old

The London Plane in March 2012

and was part of a major planting which took place in the grounds of the house. A wonderful copper beech *Fagus sylvatica 'purpurea'* was also planted at that time. It is the same height and age as the oak and has a girth of 2.95 m . It gives such wonderful spring colours in my dining room, although it does cast a dense shade, typical of the beech. It was fashionable at that time to plant copper beech in preference to the type tree. In fact, it was probably over planted as today we are seeing the results of not giving enough thought to the eventual size and spread of the tree. However, that does not apply to this specimen. I will gladly sacrifice my back garden for the splendour of the tree (although I'm not sure my wife agrees with me!!). The third of these outstanding trees is a horse-chestnut *Aesculus hippocastanum* which grows alongside the copper beech. 15 m tall with a girth of 3.53 m, it completes the trio of 130 years old trees in the wood. It is nice to see a horse-chestnut that is not ripped apart by young boys seeking conkers. Although this species is a familiar site in Britain, it is not native. It is native only to a few mountains in Greece and was not grown in western Europe until after 1600. The remainder of Oakhill Wood is younger but still of value. Other trees of note are a developing ash *Fraxinus excelsior* and an intriguing sycamore *Acer pseudoplatanus* which has an unusual shape and texture. There is also some quite old hawthorn *Crataegus monogyna* on one of the boundaries which is the remnant of an old boundary hedge. It is not easy to age this species, but I suspect that it is at least as old as the oak. Some of that is being retained as small trees, whilst the remainder is being returned to hedging.

Much planting has been carried out in recent years to ensure the continuation of the woodland and provide the interesting trees of the next century. Many neglected and rare species have been planted including the once traditional spindle *Euonymus europaea*, the scarce wild service *Sorbus torminalis* and the rare black poplar *Populus nigra*.

Moving across to Finch Way now, many fine trees have disappeared in the last ten years, including a fine old oak and a big horse-chestnut. The oldest of the surviving Brundall House trees is now a London plane *Platanus x acerifolia*. It is a giant 18 m in height with a girth of 4.39 m and is around 150 years old. London plane is not an indigenous species, being a cross between the American plane *P occidentalis* and the oriental plane *P orientalis* and being known in Britain since about 1680. This massive tree is not as old as it first appears as it enjoys quite rapid growth. It can live for up to 300 years and, as a reassurance for those people living close to this tree, the species has never been known to blow down and is rarely affected seriously by pest or disease. Just to prove that Tree Wardens are not the only people to enthuse about trees, Roman orators and statesmen used to travel home at lunch time just to feed wine to their plane trees. Now, I love trees but that's taking things just a bit too far. Personally, I'd drink the wine myself as I talk to the tree! The great commander Xerxes stopped his army of nearly two million men just to admire a certain plane tree, then covered it with precious metals and gems. Yes, well!

Moving on further, the lower end of the Finch way estate has been grossly undervalued. There are no major trees remaining there in the normal sense of the word, but some of the coppice stools are very old. What appears at first sight to be shrubby, small hazel and lime bushes are actually old coppice stools. Look closer and you will see that the shoots all come from a common base. The shoots above the ground may be only a few years old, but the roots under the ground are considerably older than that and if they had not been coppiced, I would probably be writing about the giant limes that grow there. It must always be remembered that size is not always an indication of old age. Luckily, during 2005, the residents of the Finch Way estate, the Atlantica Residents Ltd, entered into a joint project with Brundall Parish Council to manage and preserve these vulnerable trees and shrubs and they are safer now than they have been for many years.

In addition to those areas already covered, Brundall House trees also exist at the bottom of the rear Gardens of numbers 47b and 47c The Street. You can also find survivors in the gardens of some of the properties on Deepdale. These are predominantly sycamore with some oak. None are of any great age yet, but they may be one day if they are allowed to develop. I regret that I never saw Brundall House. It was demolished before I moved to Brundall. Some say that it wasn't really a nice property and others are sad that it has gone Whatever your view, it was a major house in the history of Brundall and, as such, it must be afforded the respect it demands. Perhaps it is a reflection of modern society that Brundall House was no longer needed. The days of such properties are gone and we needed the space it occupied for a different purpose. Similarly, we are finding new uses for the space occupied by the trees of Brundall House and therefore the chainsaw is gradually removing them. That grand era of Brundall House has passed, but it must not be forgotten. For me, it will live on in the trees that remain and the picture of it in its glorious prime that I have in my imagination.

One final, uncanny point regarding the history of Brundall House. Elisha de Hague, who built the house, died there on 11 November 1826. The house was demolished on 11 November 1969! The historical data on Brundall and Brundall House is taken from "A Concise History of Brundall

The London Plane with all its leaves August 2012

and Braydeston" by the late G J Levine. It is a most interesting booklet and I recommend it to anyone interested in the history of our village. It is available from Brundall and Braydeston churches for a nominal sum. Alternatively, I will be pleased to obtain copies for anyone wishing to purchase one. All profits are shared between the funds of the two churches.

*

7

'The William Coleman Limes'

7

The William Coleman Limes

AS we have seen from the previous Chapter, the most important house in the parish was Brundall House. In 1896, the property was bought by William Coleman and it is then that the story of the William Coleman Limes begins. William Coleman invented Wincarnis in 1887 and it was that invention that made his "fortune". As well as purchasing Brundall House, Coleman also acquired much land in Brundall. However, in 1900 he became financially involved and his trustees sold the house to Henry ffiske. Fortunately, Coleman's finances recovered and in 1906 he re-purchased the house from Henry ffiske at a higher price than he sold it. However, his recovery was short-lived and a recurrence of his financial troubles forced him to move to "Riverscourt" in 1912. Further money troubles compelled him to then retire to "Inglebank" where he died in very straitened circumstances in 1918.

Coleman bought the house at a time when it appears to have been fashionable to move to Brundall. When one looks at the increase in population that time, you can see that this was the place to be. Between the 1891 and 1901 censuses, the population of the parish remained constant at 347. By 1911 it had risen to 490, an increase of 41%. The next ten years saw a further 29% increase to 633. It was the start of the gradual growth of Brundall that would continue to the present day. During his occupancy of Brundall House, Coleman decided that the entrance was not grand enough for his taste. As I said earlier, he also purchased much land in the parish, among which was the land opposite the house, stretching to the northern end of Cucumber Lane. He had a road constructed across those fields. The large gate posts at "Northlace", on the northern side of the roundabout at the top of Finch Way, once supported an arch which complemented a similar arch in the wall of Brundall House. Coleman also constructed a pair of gate houses, one either side of his grand driveway, and they survive today opposite the Memorial Hall. The other end of the road, the start of Coleman's new grand driveway to his house, was lined with an avenue of common limes *Tilia x europaea*, the twelve survivors of which today form The William Coleman

The Limes opposite Finch Way February 2012

The Limes entrance in Cucumber Lane January 2006

Limes. The common lime is a hybrid between our two native limes, the broad-leaved lime *Tilia platyphylos* and the small-leaved lime *Tilia cordata*, but is probably not native itself. It is the common lime for streets and long avenues and is the worst tree known for either purpose. It does achieve a great height, up to 46m and lives long, 400 years or more, but its roots are invasive.

I feel really sorry for poor old William Coleman. It appears that he tried hard, but just could not sustain his position. I guess it boils down to the fact that he had grand ideas beyond his means. Having said that, he has left a lasting memento of his occupancy of that wonderful old house. The William Coleman Limes have not yet lived anywhere near their expected lifespan and therefore, given continued good health, should continue to give us pleasure for many years to come. In addition, they are protected by a Tree Preservation Order.

Of course, in keeping with his habit of not quite getting it right, Coleman never saw the full beauty of his avenue. He died when the trees were only twenty years old and about 10 m tall. Today they stand a mighty 25 m in height with trunks of 2.2 m girth and they are still growing. His idea was a very good one though. Looking at the trees today, it is easy to miss the intention. They appear to be just two lines of trees. However, take the time to look between them. Look down Coleman's Avenue and imagine the view. No buildings between you and Brundall House. You would enter a winding avenue of tall, impressive limes giving a wonderful overhead canopy. Imagine the incredible colours and lighting effects that would filter through. The softening of the sounds by the foliage. It would have been a grand site. Add a horse and carriage and............well, I leave it to you.

I like to imagine Brundall House in all its glory, with the breathtaking Brundall Gardens down the road. Add the centre of the village, as it was at that time, around the Rectory with the village pond opposite and it must have really been something special. I would like to have met William Coleman as well. He deserved better but appears to have been doomed to fail. Anyway, thank you Mr Coleman. Thank you for The William Coleman Limes.

*

8

'The Princess Diana Tree'

8

The Princess Diana Tree

A TREE doesn't have to be old to be interesting, nor does it have to be very large. So far in this series we have looked at old and large trees. However, Brundall has a very interesting tree that was only planted in March 1998. It is a tree that commemorates the life of Diana Princess of Wales. I will never forget waking on that awful morning to sombre music being played on Radio Broadland. As I waited for the news bulletin, I wondered if the DJ had a severe headache or something. It was so out of character. Then, of course, the news reader spoke those terrible words, "It is with deep regret that Radio Broadland announces the death of Diana Princess of Wales." I will always remember that.

I have no hesitation in admitting that I was an admirer of that exceptional young woman. The world is a poorer place without her. The warmth of that smile, the gentle touch and that wicked glint in the corner of her eye. Oh yes, she will be sadly missed for a long time. She was a ray of sunshine in our lives and so many of the people privileged to have met her will forever cherish the moment. It would be easy to be sidetracked into writing about the way the press suddenly put her on a pedestal and hailed her as the woman of the Millennium such a short time after hounding her and finding any little thing to criticise. I will leave it to others to consider that. Instead, I will concentrate on why Brundall chose to commemorate her short life.

Broadland District Council decided that it would be a fitting tribute to supply each of the 65 parishes with a tree. The choice of species and location were left to the parishes themselves. Brundall Parish Council did not hesitate to accept the offer, and I was charged with organising matters, something which I regarded as a privilege. I chose a flowering wild cherry *Prunus avium 'plena'*, because it is indigenous and displays different attractions according to the season. It is a beautiful spreading tree with masses of double, pure white flowers in spring. In autumn, the dark green foliage turns an attractive red. It represents how I saw Diana, Princess of Wales.

On Sunday 1st March 1998, around sixty villagers assembled at the entrance to the car park on The Street. It was a lovely afternoon, six months after Diana's death. Kaya Bath and Joshua Harbord, the oldest girl and youngest boy from Brundall County Primary School, chosen to reflect Diana's close affinity with children, planted the tree on behalf of the village. With the planting completed, Ian Witard, Chairman of Brundall Parish Council, presented them with commemorative certificates especially designed for the occasion. Councillor George Debbage, Chairman of Broadland District Council, then made the following speech:-

"Good afternoon ladies and gentlemen, boys and girls. Can I thank you all for inviting me here today to this special occasion to commemorate the life of Diana Princess of Wales. The Council felt that by offering each of the 65 parishes within the Broadland District the opportunity to plant a tree of their choice, this would be a fitting tribute as well as a living memorial to Diana - someone who was a very special person who endeared herself to the nation by her love and care for others. I am equally honoured to say that following the planting of the first tree in Thorpe St Andrew, the Council received two very nice letters, one from Buckingham Palace and the other from Earl Spencer, both thanking the Council for this gesture. Your own Parish gesture of complementing today's planting with a special service is, I believe, unique, but I am sure you will agree equally deserving for such a unique and special person as Diana, Princess of Wales."

The Reverend Richard Espin-Bradley of St Laurence Church then gave the following address:-

"My guess is that almost every one of us here, from the youngest to the oldest, will be able to remember where they were, and even what they were doing, at the moment they heard the news of the tragic death of Diana, Princess of Wales. It was one of those unexpected and shocking events - like the Hillsborough football stadium disaster and the Dunblane school massacre - which make a lasting impression on us. Of course, one reason why Diana's death prompted such an extraordinary and moving reaction was because of the sort of person she was. In the words of Her Majesty the Queen, when she spoke to the nation on the Friday after her death, Diana was 'an exceptional and gifted human being', who, 'in good times and bad, never lost her capacity to smile and laugh, nor to inspire others with her warmth and kindness.' She was also one of those people whose lives, even if not perfect, seem to be full of meaning. She had what I imagine many of us wish we had - beauty, wealth, status. And yet in an instant, while most of us slept, she left it all behind! But what Diana will be remembered for most, of course, isn't how much money she had, or the glamorous dresses she wore, but her charitable work, most notably publicising work on behalf of people with HIV/Aids, and campaigning for a ban on the manufacture and use

John Fleetwood with the oldest and youngest member of Brundall School planting the Princess Diana tree on Sunday 1st March 1998

of land mines. Her love of children was also obvious in her work - she was President of the Great Ormond Street Hospital for Sick Children. And so I hope this tree, which Kaya and Joshua have helped to plant today, will be an abiding reminder of someone who, despite her imperfections, was a devoted mother, and who from a position of privilege, gave generously of herself to help others who were less fortunate. And I hope that her memory will be an inspiration to all of us. But another reason why we all felt such a sense of horror and disbelief at Diana's death was that it all seemed so unfair that someone who had so much to give, and was admired by so many, had to die so young. And I guess some of us have found ourselves asking 'Why?'. In Jerusalem, in Jesus' time, there were similar incidents of tragedy which touched and fascinated people in the same way, as theses things often do. We read about them in Luke's Gospel (chapter 13, v1-5). Some Galileans had come to Jerusalem for a religious festival and - for whatever reason - the Governor, Pontius Pilate, had had them massacred. Another time, a tower had collapsed, killing eighteen people. Like the death of Diana, these were headline tragedies in their day, which prompted people to ask 'Why?'. Why would God allow people to be killed in this way? Was it perhaps because their lives weren't all they seemed to be? Perhaps there were scandals we didn't know about. But Jesus' reply to the crowds made it clear that these were just ordinary people. They didn't die because they were special, or because they were worse than anyone else. They died because these things happen. And Jesus went on to point out that shocking and sudden tragedies like these aren't intended to be the mark of judgement on a particular life, but a reminder to all of us of both the frailty of human existence, and the fact that when we die, our lives will be subjected to divine scrutiny; 'unless you repent you will all perish as they did', (Luke 13 v 3,5). Six months on from Diana's death, I wonder how many of us have asked ourselves the question, 'Am I prepared for my death, and what lies beyond it?'. None of us can predict our own death, but we can do something about where we stand with God. We can repent, Jesus says - which means to turn away from everything we know to be wrong, and turn to him, receiving the gift of forgiveness and eternal life which he made possible by his death, on a tree, 2,000 years ago. And so as well as being a reminder of Diana, I hope that for us, and for generations still to come, it will also be a helpful reminder to make the one decision in life that really matters, so that our death, when it comes, won't really be a death at all, but a passing into eternal life."

Following the Rev Espin-Bradley's address, he led the villagers in prayers for Diana and thanks for her life. The final act of the event was the erection of a commemorative brass plaque which carries the following inscription.

This Wild Cherry *Prunus avium Plena*, supplied by Broadland District Council, was planted to commemo-

rate the life of DIANA PRINCESS
OF WALES. It was planted by Kaya
Bath and Joshua Harbord of Brun-
dall County Primary School on 1
March 1998.

The April edition of the Parish Magazine carried a full transcript of
the Rev Richard Espin-Bradley's address. Some weeks later, the Parish
Council added a seat surrounding the tree to complete Brundall's memorial.
In years to come Kaya and Joshua will be able to sit there with their respec-
tive children and grandchildren and tell them of the day they led the village
in its tribute to a quite remarkable human being. This was a very good idea
of Broadland District Council. It was a first-class initiative and it must be
noted that, at a time when Earl Spencer was fighting to prevent "tasteless"
memorials to his sister, he wrote to the Council to thank them and give his
approval. In addition, it also met with the full approval, and thanks, of
Buckingham Palace. It is fashionable to criticize the establishment and local
authorities appear to be in a "no-win" situation, but Broadland District
Council is a fine authority and this idea deserved full credit.

There is no doubt that this tree has deep meaning for me. However, I
cannot say that it is my favourite tree because I so wish that it didn't have to
be planted. Having said that, it was planted to commemorate Diana's life
and as such I find it blazes bright light and colour whenever I pass it. I cannot pass it without taking a glance and remembering; and wondering what
more Diana might have achieved had she not been involved in that accident.

The Margery Palmer Oak is a grand tree, as is the Rectory Oak. The
William Coleman Limes have so much meaning and I love looking out of my
window at the majestic Parish Boundary Oaks. However, none of them has
the personal meaning that this young cherry has. I will enjoy the tree's blos-
som each spring, when it will remind me of Diana's radiant smile. I will
watch it mature, just as the nation watched Diana mature from that shy
young kindergarten helper into a beautiful Princess. Come the autumn, the
leaves will change colour, but still be striking, just as Diana shied away from
the relentless publicity that always hounded her, but still managed to retain
her dignity as she glanced at the cameras from the corner of her eye with her
head bowed. The tree was planted by two children and we will all retain our
own image of her among children, nearly always tragically disadvantaged
children. That was the mark of her warmth. She touched those children.
No, she did more than that. She cuddled those children, as she would her

The Princess Diana Tree September 2012

own young Princes. She became their fairytale Princess and they loved her. No matter how sick, injured or deprived, she made them smile. But above all she ensured that they retained their dignity. I remember her being filmed with land mine child victims. She ensured that the cameramen captured the missing limbs because she wanted us all to appreciate just what those weapons can do, but then, as the flashing cameras began to worry the children she called a halt, quietly but firmly saying "that's enough" and giving the children a reassuring hug.

I would be most interested to read what the Parish Tree Warden will say about this tree in, say, 3,000. He (or she) will be writing about the fine cherry in the centre of the village, planted to commemorate Diana's life. What will be said of her? How will history deal with her? In many ways she was too good to be true. It is up to Kaya and Joshua to ensure that their children and grandchildren learn all about the beautiful young Princess who loved little children. Once upon a time....................

*

9

''Brundall Gardens'

9

Brundall Gardens

BRUNDALL Gardens are a very large part of Brundall's history and the result of one man's incredible vision and dedication. The Gardens were laid out in the 1880's by Dr Michael Beverley, a well-known General Practitioner and former famous citizen of Norwich. For over sixty years he was connected with the Norfolk and Norwich Hospital and for a time was Chairman of the Board of Management.

The original Gardens comprised some seventy six acres, stretching as far east as The Ram public house. Alas, what remains of those original Gardens today are far less extensive and glorious than when Dr Beverley created them. At its peak, from about 1889 until the mid-1930's, Brundall Gardens was one of the most popular, spectacular and cultivated beauty spots in East Anglia. No fewer than 60,000 people visited the site in 1922, travelling by rail, by river, by bicycle and on foot. Very few travelled by motor car.

The sad story of the decline and fall of Brundall Gardens, which began soon after the departure of the Stringer family, the last occupants of Redclyffe House, is well-known to local folk. The Stringers left in 1968. Those last years of Brundall Gardens as a substantial private estate were characterised by dissension and sordid dispute as to what its precise future should be. It has been so sad to watch the Gardens gradually overtaken by invasive species and untamed nature. The Gardens were not natural, but created by man. Therefore, they depended on continued management by man if they were to survive. The main features of Beverley's creation were his arboretum and the series of three terraced ponds descending to a 4 acre mere. His vision was, without doubt, exceptional. The unique combination of the, then, existing Brundall Wood and the many introduced specimen tree species from far flung corners of the globe gave a truly spectacular backdrop to the water feature.

Established, as they are now, and towering sometimes at heights of almost 27m (90 feet) above the steep slopes of the Gardens and the mere

3367 THE ENTRANCE, BRUNDALL GARDENS

Entrance to Brundall Gardens early 20th Century

below, it requires a quite deliberate act of imagination to realise the vision that Beverley must have possessed. The redwoods *Sequoia* tower dominantly above the remainder of the canopy, while the cedars *Cedrus* command your attention. In autumn, the maples *Acer* stand out as their foliage takes on that deep red hue before finally falling. Add to those the majesty of the oaks *Quercus*, the longevity of the yew *Taxus* and the beauty of the weeping willow *Salix*, ash *Fraxinus* and beech *Fagus*. Beverley had to imagine how they would all sit together and he truly had the eye of an artist and visionary.

At the base of the steep valley, known as The Dock, Beverley constructed his water feature and to the east of that he constructed a log cabin house, a special and substantial place. During the creation of the ponds, dug out of a cleft in the ground, which was probably eroded by land springs which still exist, evidence of Roman occupation of the site was discovered. Beverley found large quantities of clay lump, charcoal, carbonised wood and, further west, a heap of unburnt clay bricks. After the archaeologist Fox had scrutinised the "finds" and pronounced that it was probable that they were evidence of Roman boat-building or boat repair activities, Beverley advanced the theory that he had discovered the remains of a Roman Dock. Unfortunately, as wonderful as it would be for it to be true, his theory was based on the scantiest of evidence. A few large wooden spars, nails and other materials are not inconclusive proof of ancient boat building. The excavations were casual and inconclusive and left a number of questions unanswered. What is more, it is unlikely that those questions will ever be answered fully. It is true that the area was known as Dock Close in 1839, but the possibility that the word "Dock" may have applied to the wild plant of that name should not be overlooked. The late G J Levine suggested, in his excellent booklet "A Concise History of Brundall and Braydeston", that it seems probable that the site was occupied by a Roman brick and tile maker who lived in the villa, the remains of which was discovered near the road and opposite Brundall Service Station. Foundations, roofing tiles, bricks and fragments of domestic pottery were unearthed.

After the Romans left this country, the site was definitely occupied by Saxons. Much Saxon pottery has been found there, including a cremation urn containing the bones and ashes of a child together with some blue glass beads. That is now in Norwich Castle Museum. The Roman Dock theory had a final act when, following the commencement of the development of part of Brundall Gardens, a private road was named Roman Drive.

In 1911, Beverley put his estate up for sale, but it was not until 1917 that there came onto the scene the second notable character who was to leave his imprimatur on the place. Beverley had been a natural scientist; precise and cautious in his approach, apparently almost to the point of pedantry. Frederick Holmes Cooper, a self-made man whose roots were in Wisbech in Cambridgeshire, was the new owner. A quietly spoken entrepreneur with vigour and his own particular kind of vision; in many ways he was a man long before his time. In these days when the opening of estates, gardens and stately homes is common-place, we have to remember just how innovative was that little pioneer, only 5 feet 5 inches tall but commanding attention and action nevertheless. He saw Brundall Gardens as a special place and he was single-minded in his ideas about developing it and sharing it with the world around him. An estate agent by profession, Cooper later became deeply involved in the burgeoning cinema industry and from Norfolk he became the leader of the British exhibitors campaigning against the invading Americans, intent on acquiring outlets for their films.

Frederick Cooper's influence in popularising and making known Brundall Gardens was enormous. People flocked to visit them in their hundreds and thousands every weekend. He was not a natural plantsman or horticulturist, but he recognised the fact and delegated the gardening activities and the detailed planning thereof to Strachan, his faithful head gardener. Eric Cooper, Frederick's son, described Strachan as "a gardener of really outstanding talent". The London and North Eastern Railway Company were persuaded by the energetic Cooper to build a halt, Brundall Gardens Railway Station, virtually at the entrance gate and trains disgorged visitors from Norwich directly into his care. To encourage visitors from the coast and the other end of the county, Cooper founded the Brundall Gardens Steamship Company. Its brochure described the scene for those visitors who travelled in the Victorious, up-river towards Brundall to visit the Gardens. "At a sharp point the stream is cut, that section on the left being the Waveney. The grey lines of ancient walls, remarkably well-preserved, mark the Roman soldiers' camp. The bricks of the walls are harder today than in AD 100." And again, "Often our boat puts up some small twittering birds from the mud of the river banks – they're Sandpipers. Herons fly up and pass in limbering flight overhead: they are after water voles, eels or shrimps............ The salt air had provoked a healthy thirst. Let's go into the cabin and have a cup of tea, a bottle of 'pop' or something stronger."

A H Patterson was the author of Cooper's call to take the river excursion up to Brundall and the Gardens, tea room, restaurant, museum and other facilities that he laid out there in his beloved retreat. Stephen Peart also describes in his book how many notable people of the film and literary

The water feature constructed by Dr Beverley known as 'The Dock'
See front cover

worlds, including Charlie Chaplin, visited and stayed at Redclyffe House when it was built by Cooper to replace Dr Beverley's log cabin house which was destroyed by fire.

As one today surveys the shores of the lake, or mere as it was called, and the remnants of those formal gardens to the east of the Dock, it is difficult to credit what ordered beauty was to be found there. Our minds cannot adjust to the attitudes of those that not only created Brundall Gardens, but worked so hard to maintain it. The gardeners in those days worked for very little reward other than the love of what they did. Is that what we lack today? Where today can we find the love and inspiration of Beverley; the commercial acumen of Cooper; the love and dedication of gardeners such as Strachan, not to mention his staff of over twenty? It is no longer a viable business proposition to run such a place as Brundall Gardens and not many people have the inclination to spend a large part of their wealth on maintaining Beverley's creation.

Dr Beverley created an arboretum of the highest quality. His claim of having planted a tree of every species was somewhat far-fetched, but he certainly planted an enormous variety. When he died in 1930, his creation had matured and he must have ended his days a contented man, having left such a wonderful asset for the village. I am pleased that he didn't see his work deteriorate as it has in recent years. Again today, it has become the centre of acrimony as plans are considered for further development at the top of the escarpment and it appears that any slim chance of the general public once again being able to enjoy the Gardens has gone forever.

In the garden of Lake House, the home of Gary and Janet Muter, one can still get a flavour of what things were like. They are to be congratulated on the hard work and financial investment they have put into preserving Dr Beverley's water feature. With their neighbours, they are ensuring that a part of Brundall Gardens will live on. I am sure that we will all thank them for that and I am equally sure that Dr Beverley will be pleased that this part of his creation has passed into such safe hands.

On a personal note, I wish to thank them for kindly allowing me to base this Chapter on their leaflet, "A Hundred Years in Brundall Gardens". You can obtain a copy of the leaflet by attending one of their regular open days when they raise funds for the National Gardens Scheme and Water Aid, both most worthwhile causes.

*

10

'Brundall's Oak'

10

Brundall's Oak

AMONG the Notable Trees of Brundall, we have seen very old trees and a very young tree. Now we have come to a very young tree raised from one of the very old trees that we've already seen. In addition, Brundall's Oak has a lovely story to tell. In 1998, I approached David Capp, the then Head Teacher at Brundall School, to ask if the school would be interested in raising trees to be planted out to celebrate the forthcoming Millennium. The idea was a community project involving children that could also be put to educational use. To my delight, David was most enthusiastic and that led to the Brundall Millennium Tree Planting Project where children from the school joined David and me to collect acorns from the Parish Boundary Oaks described in Chapter 4. We then potted them up and raised trees to be planted out around the village. It was most successful and extremely enjoyable. The children all had green fingers and I soon had a crop of healthy seedlings which, once they were ready, I planted around the village. Indeed, all were planted out except for one which I finally put in Oakhill Wood at the rear of my house. Sadly, toward the end of 2002, I stood at my front door and watched in horror as one of those boundary oaks blew apart in a terrible gale. It was a hollow specimen with tons of character but also, alas, evidence of bracket fungi. Over a period of thirty minutes or so, I watched it become so dangerous that what was left would have to be felled. Luckily, of course, it just so happened that I had that one young oak left. Being a descendent of the tree we lost, it would make the ideal replacement, having the perfect provenance. The second generation of boundary oaks was about to begin.

Before I could approach Broadland District Council and offer the young tree as a suitable replacement for planting on their land, I heard the sad news that one of the real characters of our village had passed away. He was well-loved by everyone he met and, in particular, that old man was so popular with children. Probably, one of those children who liked him so much was the very child whose acorn raised the tree I was thinking of planting. So, why not make it a commemorative tree as well as a replacement for that mighty old oak we had lost? If trees have a meaning or purpose, they have so much more chance of surviving the pressures of the 21st century and beyond.

To me, that old oak was so important as a part of the village history so its replacement could only honour someone very special in Brundall. The very special person wasn't a person at all though................ He was a little dog called Brundall!!! Brundall had a real story to tell. Not just because he was named Brundall but because he was so loved by just about everyone. This is Brundall's story, based on details supplied by his owner, his Mum, Hilda Taylor. Are you sitting comfortably? Have you got the Kleenex ready? Then I'll begin:-

"Shall we go home?". The words, unspoken, which had hung in the air for several days were finally out and quietly agreed. The weather had been absolutely awful. Sadly, Ron and Hilda Taylor loaded their car and turned their backs on the village of Brundall. They returned home to Kent on Friday, two whole days before the planned end of their holiday. They knew how wonderful a Broads holiday could be, but that in May 1987 had just been rain, mud, a leaking boat and the resultant wet duvets and beds. Combined with minor illnesses, it all conspired to make it a miserable time. So, they began their sad journey back to Kent, little knowing that they were experiencing one of those life changing days which happen in all lives. By 9:00pm they had unpacked, had a few conciliatory drinks, and were sitting having their evening meal. For the first time for a week they were feeling dry, warm and relaxed. Suddenly, there came the sound of dreadful crying and howling from outside. Ron thought that it was an injured fox, many of which frequented their home area. Hilda went outside to investigate and found a tiny puppy madly scratching on the fence to attempt to get back to whatever represented security in its short life. It was clear that the puppy had been dumped. The rear garden was entirely enclosed by high fencing and the only access point was the public road alongside the garden. Hilda went inside and told Ron that it was a puppy, dumped in the garden. Ron's reply was "Well, you'd better bring it in". Fate had taken its first turn! After giving the puppy a reassuring cuddle, they rang Gravesend police station to report what had happened. The police were very kind and suggested that they took the dog to the police station where it would be kept overnight and delivered to an Animal Rescue Centre in the morning. Trouble was that Ron and Hilda had been consoling themselves with those drinks. They therefore

Brundall's Oak August 2012

suggested to the police that they might prefer it if they didn't drive that night and agreed to look after the little fellow overnight. They planned to take it to the station in the morning. Their fate was sealed!

Why is it that a puppy, after a night of whimpering, crying, whinging and desperation to get back to its mum, has already captivated your heart, not to mention shared your bed? Suffice it to say that the visit the following morning was not to the police, but for a check out at the local vet!! The puppy was a butch little dog, long and low, a tricolour mongrel with a most endearing personality. The name came immediately – BRUNDALL. It was very likely that he would have spent the wet and cold night in the garden had Ron and Hilda not curtailed their holiday. Indeed, he would have possibly died. Brundall enchanted everyone he met and he adored children. He was such a lively, happy, active, little dog. Many who knew him will remember his habit of dashing to the top of the stairs when anyone arrived and dropping down the stairs one of his many balls. He taught so many people his game of catching the ball at the top, and then nosing it down for them to throw again. A game he would play constantly, teaching it to every new visitor, whether they were really interested or not. Friends would initially hesitate when told that Ron and Hilda would leave their parties after four hours to go home to their dog, "Unless, of course, we might bring him with us?". Eventually, friends would invite him enthusiastically, sometimes in preference to the Taylors themselves! It was very simple. Brundall had changed their lives. They found it impossible to put him into kennels and, although friends were more than willing to care for him while they went away, Ron and Hilda were never very happy top be apart from him So, foreign holidays were the first casualty!

As an alternative to foreign trips, the Taylors purchased a boat. Needless to say, they moored it in Brundall! Where else? It also gave little Brundall another opportunity to enchant people. Ron and Hilda had so much to thank him for. Each weekend they would travel with him from Kent to Norfolk. People would make a fuss of Brundall, especially in the Yare pub. Ask his name, as people do, and immediately a lengthy conversation ensued. Brundall made Ron and Hilda so many very valued and long term friends because of his character and his name. Brundall saw his devoted owners through the 1987 Great Storm, witnessed the virtual rebuilding of their home, sat with them whilst they anguished over the first Gulf War, was with them through good and bad times. He was always happy, always ready for a walk and play. It was a regret that, throughout his life, he never achieved his life's ambition. That was to have two toys in his mouth simultaneously!

Mind you, it wasn't for want of trying!!

Then, in 1995, came redundancy for Ron and the resultant decision to move house from Kent to Brundall. Sadly, things went badly from then. Ron had a serious illness diagnosed shortly after they arrived and died within a year. The years took their toll and Brundall slowed down, but he was still always there for Hilda; always a distraction; always able to lift spirits and provoke a smile. Above all though, Brundall was always a friend. He seemed to stay around to watch over Hilda until she achieved a semblance of a new life. He became so well known in the village. Not just with his drinking pals at the Yare. Yes, Hilda had to take him there regularly to quench his thirst. No, he also became a big favourite with the local children, being so gentle with them. Sadly though, Brundall was aging rapidly and the old chap died just before Christmas 2002, at almost 16 years of age.

Today, Brundall's oak can look forward to several hundred years of life given the care and respect it deserves. It sits proudly on the area of amenity land on Oakhill, alongside the stump of its parent. The children that so loved Brundall pass it every day on their way to school. There is a postscript to Brundall's story. Through friends in Brundall Ron and Hilda met Jan and Jose, Dutch people who became good friends. Jan retired from the Amsterdam Fire Service in 2,000 and decided that they could now look after a dog. On a visit to Brundall a few months before he retired, Jan tentatively asked Hilda, since they loved Norfolk and especially Brundall Village so much, whether she would object to them calling their new dog "Brundall". So Brundall's story goes on…in the shape of a much loved hunting dog living in Friesland, Holland!

'Brothers and sisters, I bid you beware of giving your heart,
to a dog, to tear…'. Kipling.

*

11

'Brundall Church Fen
Local Nature Reserve'

11

Brundall Church Fen Local Nature Reserve

WELCOME to Brundall Church Fen Local Nature Reserve. Brundall Parish Council is delighted to be working in close co-operation with Norfolk County Council and the Broads Authority to manage this wonderful site. Brundall Parish Council purchased Brundall Church Fen in March 1980 from Mrs H F Geary. It is situated to the south of St Laurence Church and is accessed via Church Lane. Lying to the east of Brundall Broad, between the railway and the River Yare, the site comprises some 3.133 hectare (7.743 acres) of fen and alder carr and is an area of former grazing marsh, forming part of the flood plain of the River Yare.

Faden's Map of 1797 shows the entire flood plain area of Brundall as fen or marsh. The first edition Ordnance Survey Map of 1838 indicates the area as grazing land. By 1908, a few patches of mixed woodland were present, with a strip of woodland adjacent to the upland margins. In the 1980s, two "roadways" crossed the site, following the route of the current boardwalk and main footpath, with the land between them being denoted "meadow". Owing to the gradual decline of grazing during the 20th century, the site has seen extensive scrub and carr woodland development. It remained unmanaged for several years and that helped it to become the jewel it is today.

In 1998, Brundall Parish Council took the bold decision to create a conservation area at Brundall Church Fen whilst still providing a public amenity area. It was not an easy task, balancing the interests of the various user groups, but the Council gradually succeeded, encouraging them to work in harmony. The Broads Authority was most supportive and provided practical help and advice. Without that expertise and encouragement the task would have been all the more daunting. Then, on 21 July 2003, Brundall Church Fen was officially granted the status of a Local Nature Reserve (LNR) following the signing of an Agreement between Brundall Parish Council, English Nature and Norfolk County Council, and its management passed into the safe hands of a dedicated Management Committee.

Without doubt, it is because the site was "neglected" for so many

Church Fen April 2012

years that it is so important today. It was not subjected to the "management" carried out so unsympathetically during recent decades. One of the problems many such sites have suffered from is that people want woodland to be tidy. Luckily, Brundall Church Fen is far from that and it will remain in its current "natural" state that makes it so valuable. Many woodland wildlife species depend on large old trees, standing dead wood and large fallen trunks and limbs. We need standing dead wood for insects to inhabit and those insects are a food source for our bird populations. Standing dead trees play host to numerous wood-rotting fungi and holes in them are used by owls and bats. They soon become covered with lichens. When they eventually fall to the ground, a new set of insect species inhabit the decaying wood, more species of wood-rotting fungi take over and different lichens cover the slowly rotting trunk.

Of course, one has to consider public safety when retaining standing deadwood and that is why public access to Brundall Church Fen Local Nature Reserve is restricted to the designated pathways and boardwalks only. By making such a restriction, we are able to retain fine examples old standing dead trees and numerous fallen and wind-blown trees left intact to rot down naturally. Several of our fallen and wind-blown willows have now re-rooted and second generation trees are growing from the fallen ones. The visitor can see examples of very large wind-blown willows that have continued to live on and now have fresh, vigorous growth shooting from their mighty, fallen, moss-covered trunks.

One of Brundall Church Fen's best attractions has to be the large reed bed. Occupying the centre of the site, the public are not permitted to access it. However, fine views may be obtained from a number of points. Accessing the reed bed is dangerous, even for trained and experienced personnel. Cutting is carried out sympathetically in order to encourage a more species-rich environment. It is a truly wonderful sight to watch a heron glide over the reed bed on a misty evening.

As stated earlier, Brundall Church Fen will never be neat and tidy and it will never become a play area. Having said that, the local Brownies, Guides, Scouts and Cubs make extensive use of the facilities to earn environmental badges, etc. Brundall Church Fen is also an important amenity area within the village and the Management Committee is always mindful of the requirements of such users. Anglers have always used the site and they will be encouraged to continue to do so. In addition, it is a popular place for weekend walkers with many families enjoying a Sunday afternoon stroll with the dog. There is no reason why Brundall Church Fen should not fulfill the

Church Fen May 2012

purposes of both a Local Nature Reserve and a local amenity area. Users just need to exercise some thought and respect for both the site and each other. The Broads Authority maintain 24-hour moorings on the river bank, providing a beautiful amenity for those holiday makers and boating enthusiasts seeking a more peaceful and natural spot to spend the night.

An abundance of wildlife freely inhabits Brundall Church Fen, including Chinese water deer, foxes and water vole. However, the most exciting fact is that otter has been seen on several occasions. Needless to say, the Management Committee will do all it can to provide a safe habitat for the otter and afford it the maximum protection possible from the predatory mink that inhabits the river banks.

A formal Management Plan has been agreed for the site and is available for public inspection on request to the Clerk to Brundall Parish Council. When visiting Brundall Church Fen, please be considerate. Take your litter home with you. Remember that it is a Local Nature Reserve. Small creatures easily become trapped inside discarded bread bags or tin cans and, as a result, die a slow death. Obviously, fires are not permitted because, whilst the site is by nature wet, in summer months the northern wooded area plus the dried out sections of the site become a tinder-box.

Enjoy the delights of Brundall Church Fen Local Nature Reserve...................It's free!!

*

12

'From our Archives'

IN CONCLUSION

WE CONCLUDE with a few photographs of tree related events from Brundall Local History Group's archives. These span about 25 years, from the gales of 1987 which did so much damage to our trees, to a guided walk we had with the tree warden in 2011, and the planting of a tree in memory of Joan Adams in 2012.

At the millennium a service was held in Brundall Churchyard by the rector, Bob Baker, at which a yew tree was planted. The tree was a cutting from one in Palestine that dated from the birth of Christ.

Planting a yew tree in the churchyard 2nd April 2000 to commemorate the Millenium. John Evans, Group Leader of Brundall Scouts with the plant

Storm damage to some trees in St. Laurence Avenue in the great gale in October 1987

The thatched summerhouse at no. 88 The Street destroyed in the great gale of October 1987

A walk with the Tree Warden in June 2011
Learning about the robinia tree outside 'The Lavender House'

John Adams adding soil to the Rowan Tree planted in memory of his wife, Joan, in April 2012

This tree is planted in memory of

JOAN ADAMS 1931–2011

Parish Clerk from 1976 to 1996

and valued member of

Brundall Local History Group

14th April 2012